The Life Cycle of Water Plants

by Gary Rushworth

Table of Contents

Introduction 2
Chapter 1 What Are Water Plants? 4
Chapter 2 How Water Plants Grow 10
Chapter 3 Water Plant Reproduction 16
Conclusion 21
Solve This Answers 22
Glossary 23
Index 24

Introduction

When we think of plants, we usually think about plants that grow in soil. Did you know that many plants don't grow in soil at all? Some even grow entirely under the water. Water plants are similar to earth plants in some ways. They are also very different. How? Read on to find out!

▼ Water plants grow in ponds, lakes, and other bodies of water.

▲ There are many different kinds of water plants.

▲ Some water plants have roots in soil or sand.

In this book, you will read about different kinds of water plants. You will learn about what makes them like the plants we see growing above the ground. Land plants have roots that grow under the ground. Some water plants have roots that grow underground, too. Other water plants have roots that grow on rocks, or even on fish!

Did you know that some water plants grow without seeds? Other water plants float for their whole life cycle. Read on to learn about the life cycle of water plants. Jump in and let's look underwater to discover what water plants are all about!

CHAPTER 1

What Are Water Plants?

Most of the plants we are familiar with are those that grow on land. These plants are rooted in soil. Plants rooted in soil on land are called **terrestrial** (tuh-RES-tree-ul) plants. Some plants live all or most of the time in water. Plants like this are called **aquatic** (uh-KWAH-tik), or water, plants.

▲ A rose bush is a terrestrial plant.

Some aquatic plants live in fresh water. Other aquatic plants live in salt water. Some live in **brackish** water. Brackish water is a mixture of fresh water and salt water.

▲ water lilies

Water quality is important to plants and all living creatures. Some plants and animals are very sensitive to changes in their habitat. Temperature, salt content, oxygen, and the level of chemicals in the water are all important.

Salinity is the amount of salt in a body of water. Salinity directly affects the animals and plants that are able to live in the water. Some areas, like Maryland's Chesapeake Bay, are brackish water. Scientists measure the level of salinity in the Chesapeake Bay to ensure the habitat remains stable.

1. Solve This

Scientists measure salinity with a refractometer. This device measures the amount of light through a sample of water. The higher the salt content, the more the meter changes, or refracts. The salinity of fresh water is zero. The salinity of salty ocean water is near 35. If a fish needs a salinity of zero to survive, what kind of fish is it?

▲ a refractometer

MATH ✓ POINT

What steps did you take to answer the question?

CHAPTER 1

Three Types of Water Plants

Aquatic plants are divided into three main groups. The groups are **emergent**, floating, and **submerged**.

Emergent water plants are those plants that rise above the water. These plants live in shallow water along the shoreline. Water plants like this have roots in the soft mud. Examples of this type of plant are cattails, irises, and water lilies.

▲ Cattails are emergent plants.

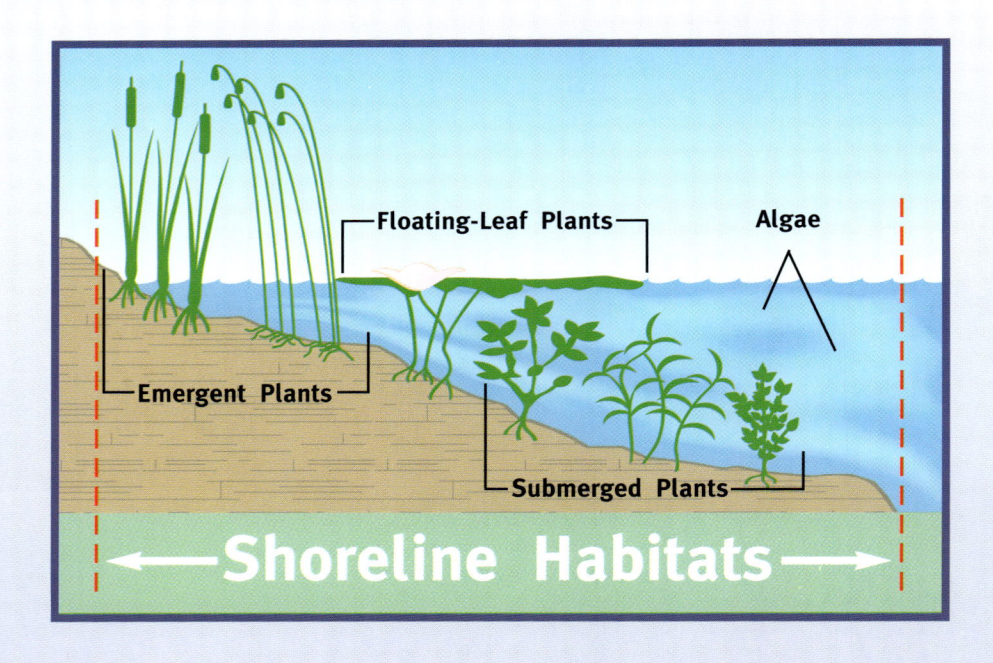

Shoreline Habitats
- Emergent Plants
- Floating-Leaf Plants
- Submerged Plants
- Algae

WHAT ARE WATER PLANTS?

◀ Some floating plants float freely in the water.

It's a Fact

Emergent water plants usually have a terrestrial, or land, ancestor. Emergent plants live in and around water. Like other plants, they need water to survive. However, they do not need to live in water to complete their life cycle.

Floating water plants, or **floaters**, float freely on or below the water's surface. Some floaters do not have roots in soil.

Submerged plants are plants that live beneath the surface of a body of water. Plants in this group are rooted in the muddy bottoms of lakes, rivers, streams, ponds, and the ocean floor. Like other plants, submerged plants need to absorb water. The water is used to make food during **photosynthesis** (foh-tuh-SIN-thuh-suhs).

✔ POINT

Visualize

Visualize a water plant you have seen. Then tell a partner whether the plant is an emergent, floating, or submerged plant and why.

CHAPTER 1

Importance of Water Plants

Water plants are important to aquatic and terrestrial habitats. Water plants are a source of food for some animals, fish, and other organisms. Water plants filter pollutants and contaminants in the water. Water plants take in dissolved carbon dioxide waste from the surrounding water. The plants change carbon dioxide into oxygen and sugar. The plants use the sugar for food. The oxygen is released into the water. This helps maintain the purity of the water.

Shoreline water plants also help prevent erosion. Erosion is the washing away of soil by heavy rains, floods, and ocean surf. Shoreline plants are the last defense against this loss. Their roots act like a net to prevent erosion.

2. SOLVE THIS

A small pond is 144 square feet (13.4 square meters). The average pond lily occupies 1 square foot (0.09 square meters). If there are 36 lily plants in the pond, what percentage of the pond is covered by lilies?

MATH ✓ POINT

How could you check your work?

WHAT ARE WATER PLANTS?

▲ Some water plants can take over a habitat.

Disadvantages of Water Plants

For all the good they do, water plants have some disadvantages, too. Water plants can be invasive. This means they can take over a habitat. Water plants can change and alter the food supply for other plants and animals.

Water plants can use up the oxygen dissolved in the water. This prevents other plants and animals from getting the oxygen they need to survive. Gradually, the water plants take over, destroying the habitat of other plants.

CHAPTER 2

How Water Plants Grow

Water plants have adapted to living in and around water. Water plants often have leaves and stems that are more flexible than those of terrestrial plants. This helps the plants move easily in the water. Some water plants have air spaces inside their stems. This helps the plants float.

Some water plants have wide leaves to help them float on the surface. Others have leaves with a waxy coating that helps repel water, making them lighter so they float.

Air spaces in the stems of some water plants help them float. ▶

▲ Plants like the lichens on these rocks do not have roots.

Plants Without Roots

All plants need water, nutrients, or food, and light to survive. Plant roots bring nutrients and water into the plant. For plants without roots, water and nutrients must be brought in through the leaves and stems.

Some water plants do not have roots in soil. These plants live on the shoreline, on the surface of the water, and under the water. They might float freely in the water or attach themselves to rocks or other plants. A few species of these plants even attach to fish and other animals.

CHAPTER 2

There are two divisions of plants. The divisions are based on how a plant gets water. The first group is made up of vascular plants. Vascular plants bring in water and nutrients through their roots. Vascular plants have water channels through their stems. The channels connect the roots of the plant under the ground with the leaves above the ground.

The second division of plants is made up of nonvascular plants. Plants without root systems fit into this variety. Nonvascular plants absorb water and nutrients through the walls of their stems and their leaves.

They Made a Difference

August Eichler (1839–1887) developed a system of plant classification. Later, Adolf Engler (1844–1930) completed the system. The system was widely used by European botanists and is still in use today.

HOW WATER PLANTS GROW

Seeds and More

The water plant life cycle begins in three ways. For some water plants, seed production is the beginning of the life cycle. Terrestrial plants begin life as seeds. Other water plants reproduce through **spores**. Spores are like seeds. Both contain the information needed to make a new plant.

Some water plants produce new plants directly from existing parent plants. This process occurs without seeds or spores. The process is called vegetative reproduction.

Water plants begin life when the seeds or spores **germinate** (JER-muh-nayt). Germination is when the plant begins to grow. Gradually, the plant grows into an adult plant capable of making more seeds or spores.

CAREERS

Plant Biologist
Botany is the study of plants. There are many kinds of plant biologists. Ecological biologists study how plant life affects the environment. Other plant biologists study how different plants are made and how they grow. To be a plant biologist, you need to study science and math.

▲ water lilies

CHAPTER 2

Photosynthesis

To grow, all new plants need to make food. This process is called photosynthesis.

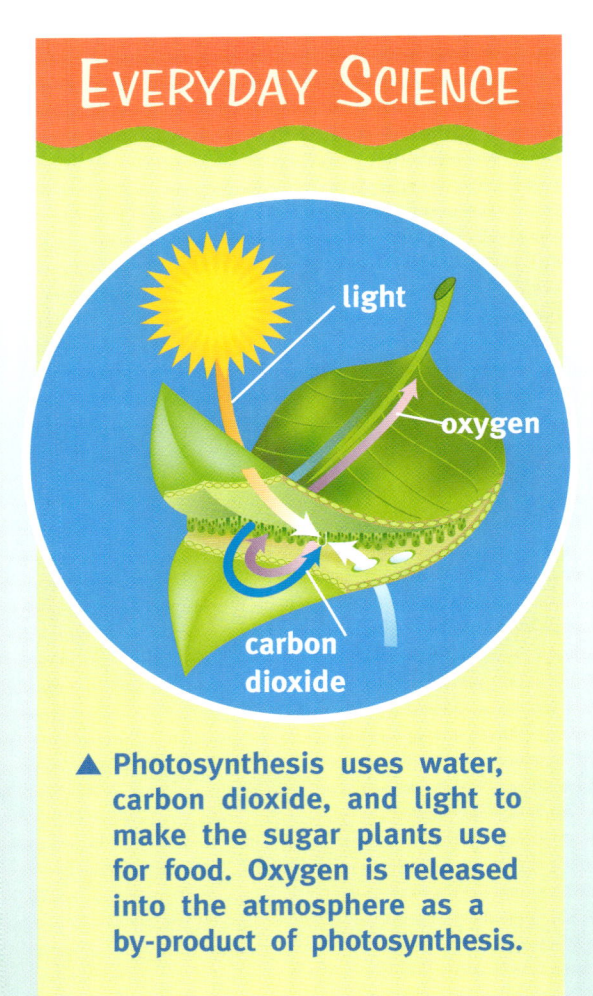

When photosynthesis happens, water, carbon dioxide, and sunlight combine to make a special sugar plants use for food. This sugar is called **glucose**. When glucose is produced, plants release oxygen into the air.

The carbon dioxide and oxygen exchange occurs underwater. Where does the oxygen come from? Humans can't breathe under water, but fish and many sea creatures do. They need oxygen to keep their cells alive. As fish swim, water passes through their gills.

EVERYDAY SCIENCE

▲ Photosynthesis uses water, carbon dioxide, and light to make the sugar plants use for food. Oxygen is released into the atmosphere as a by-product of photosynthesis.

HOW WATER PLANTS GROW

The fish remove oxygen from the water and then release carbon dioxide into the water. Underwater plants absorb the carbon dioxide and release oxygen. Underwater plants are often called **oxygenators** (ahk-sih-jeh-NAY-terz) because they help replace the oxygen in the water.

▲ underwater plant

▲ Fish help provide the carbon dioxide that water plants need to live.

CHAPTER 3

Water Plant Reproduction

Once water plants are able to make their own food, they mature into adult plants. The life cycle of a water plant ends with the production of new seeds or spores. This is also the time when vegetative reproduction begins.

Seeds, spores, and the plant itself contain all the information needed to make a new plant. We are going to look at each type of reproduction in this chapter.

▲ water plant seeds and spores

It's a Fact

Some chemicals found in soaps and fertilizers cause aquatic plants to grow faster. Aquatic plants may take over a habitat quickly. The plants use all the oxygen available and can cause fish and other plants to die. The chemicals are now regulated by laws.

◀ This is a lotus seed pod. The lotus is part of the water lily family.

Making a Seed

Most plants that produce seeds produce flowers as well. Flowers have three main parts. They are the **pistil**, the **stamen**, and the petals.

3. SOLVE THIS

Water temperature is a measure of how hot or cold water is. Water temperature changes from season to season. Water temperature also changes depending on how deep the water is. In winter, water in a pond is coldest at the surface and warmer near the bottom. Most fish and plants sense this change. Suppose the temperature of the water in a pond is 32°F (0°C) at the surface and 42°F (5.6°C) at the bottom. If a fish normally lives at a temperature of 38 to 60°F (3.3 to 15.6°C), where in the pond are you likely to find the fish?

MATH ✓ POINT

What did you need to know to solve the problem?

CHAPTER 3

Seeds develop and grow in the flower's pistil. The stamen is the part of the plant that makes pollen. Pollen is needed to make the seeds mature. The process of moving pollen from a part of the stamen to a part of the pistil is called **pollination**.

Once pollination occurs, the seeds are ready to make a new plant. The seeds remain attached to the pollen. The pollen and seeds are spread by air, water, and insects. The pollen of one plant touches a certain part on the pistil of another plant. When this happens, the seeds become fertilized, or ready to develop.

▲ parts of a flower

4. SOLVE THIS

Not all of the seeds that a plant produces grow into new plants. If a plant produces 100 seeds and only 1 of every 25 seeds produces a new plant, how many new plants will grow?

MATH ✓ POINT

How did you find your answer?

WATER PLANT REPRODUCTION

The fertilized seeds fall from the plant and begin their growth cycle. For rooted plants, this means they have to fall on sand or soil where they begin to grow their roots.

Submerged plants and water plants that do not have roots in soil form spores to make new plants. A spore is like a seed. Like seeds, spores contain the reproductive information to make a new plant. The spores are released into the water. They float until they fertilize another plant. Then, their growth cycle begins.

▲ Seeds that float are an adaptation to a water habitat.

Once fertilized, the seeds or spores germinate, or begin to grow into new water plants.

CHAPTER 3

Other water plants produce new plants through vegetative reproduction. Vegetative reproduction does not involve seeds or spores. This kind of reproduction happens when the plant simply produces new plants from its existing stems.

In vegetative reproduction, a parent plant makes new stems. A single parent plant can make many stems. The stems can become very long. Soon, there are many plants attached to the same parent plant. This group of plants is called a **colony**.

A colony can grow very large in a few years. Sometimes the colony takes over and permanently changes the habitat.

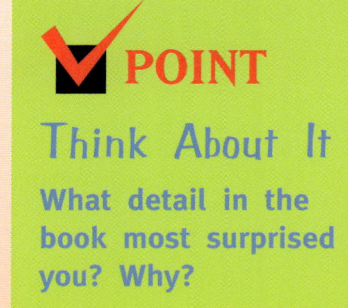

✔ POINT

Think About It
What detail in the book most surprised you? Why?

Conclusion

The plant kingdom is very large. Almost all groups within the kingdom have water plant members. New water plants are still being discovered as scientists explore lakes, rivers, streams, and oceans.

Water plants are beneficial to aquatic and terrestrial environments. Water plants are a source of food. Water plants help clean water, provide oxygen, and prevent erosion.

Aquatic plants are beneficial to water habitats. However, there must be a balance between aquatic plants, animals, and fish for the habitat to survive.

Water habitats are natural resources that need to be protected and preserved.

▲ Water plants offer animals places to hide, to reproduce, and to feed.

Solve This Answers

1. Page 5
A fish that needs a salinity of zero is a freshwater fish.

2. Page 8
25%
36 pond lilies x 1 square foot = 36
36 ÷ 144 = .25, or 25%
(36 x .09 square meters = 3.24 ÷ 13.4 = .24, or about 25%)

3. Page 17
You are more likely to find the fish at the bottom.

4. Page 18
4 plants
100 ÷ 25 = 4

Glossary

aquatic — (uh-KWAH-tik) growing or living in water (page 4)

brackish — (BRA-kish) a mixture of freshwater and salt water (page 4)

colony — (KAH-luh-nee) a group of plants living and growing together (page 20)

emergent — (ee-MER-junt) rooted shoreline plants (page 6)

floater — (FLOH-ter) a water plant with leaves that float on or below the surface of the water (page 7)

germinate — (JER-muh-nayt) to cause to grow (page 13)

glucose — (GLOO-kohs) the sugar used for food by plants (page 14)

oxygenator — (ahk-sih-juh-NAY-ter) a plant that adds oxygen to the water (page 15)

photosynthesis — (foh-toh-SIN-thuh-sus) the process plants use to make food from carbon dioxide, water, and light (page 7)

pistil — (PIS-tul) the seed-bearing part of a flower (page 17)

pollination — (pah-luh-NAY-shun) the transfer of pollen from one flower to another (page 18)

spore — (SPOR) the part of some plants that carries reproductive information (page 13)

stamen — (STAY-mun) the pollen-bearing part of a flower (page 17)

submerged — (sub-MERJD) covered with water (page 6)

terrestrial — (tuh-RES-tree-ul) land-based plants (page 4)

Index

aquatic, 4, 6, 8, 21
brackish, 4–5
carbon dioxide, 8, 14–15
colony, 20
emergent, 6–7
fertilized, 18–19
floater, 7
germinate, 13, 19
glucose, 14
nonvascular, 12
oxygenator, 15
petals, 17–18
photosynthesis, 7, 14
pistil, 17–18
pollination, 18
seed, 3, 13, 16–20
spore, 13, 16, 19–20
stamen, 17–18
submerged, 6–7, 19
terrestrial, 4, 8, 10, 13, 21
vascular, 12
vegetative reproduction, 13, 16, 20